T0137581

SALVATION

What Must I Do To Be Saved?

And he said unto them, Go ye into all the world, and preach the gospel to every creature. 16 He that believeth and is baptized shall be saved; but he that believeth not shall be damned -Mark 16:15-16

And Jesus came and spake unto them, saying, All power is given unto me in heaven and in earth. 19 Go ye therefore, and teach all nations, baptizing them in the name of the Father, and of the Son, and of the Holy Ghost: 20 Teaching them to observe all things whatsoever I have commanded you: and, lo, I am with you alway, even unto the end of the world. Amen. -Matthew 28:18-20

"Thou wast slain, and hast redeemed us to God by thy blood out of every kindred, and tongue, and people, and nation." –Revelation 5:9

Ovit G. Pursley Ministries®

Ovit G. Pursley, Sr.

First Edition
First Printing 2011

Ovit G. Pursley, Sr. Ministries®
11130 Kingston Pike Suite 103
Knoxville, Tennessee 37934

Order this book online at www.trafford.com
or email orders@trafford.com

Most Trafford titles are also available at major online book retailers.

Printed in the United States of America.

ISBN: 978-1-4269-5541-9 (sc)
ISBN: 978-1-4269-5540-2 (e)

Trafford rev. 08/27/2011

 www.trafford.com

North America & international
toll-free: 1 888 232 4444 (USA & Canada)
phone: 250 383 6864 ♦ fax: 812 355 4082

SALVATION

What Must I Do To Be Saved?

OVIT G. PURSLEY, SR.

TABLE OF CONTENTS

CHAPTER 1

Salvation

Who Shall Not Inherit the Kingdom of God?

Now the works of the flesh are manifest, which are these; Adultery, fornication, uncleanness, lasciviousness, 20 Idolatry, witchcraft, hatred, variance, emulations, wrath, strife, seditions, heresies, 21 Envyings, murders, drunkenness, revellings, and such like: of the which I tell you before, as I have also told you in time past, that they which do such things shall not inherit the kingdom of God. -Galatians 5:19-21

...They which do such things shall not inherit the kingdom of God. –Galatians 5:21

A.	Adultery	Galatians 5:19
B.	Fornication	Galatians 5:19
C.	Uncleanness	Galatians 5:19
D.	Lasciviousness	Galatians 5:19
E.	Idolatry	Galatians 5:20
F.	Witchcraft	Galatians 5:20
G.	Hatred	Galatians 5:20
H.	Variance	Galatians 5:20
I.	Emulation's	Galatians 5:20
J.	Strife	Galatians 5:20
K.	Sedition	Galatians 5:20
L.	Heresies	Galatians 5:20
M.	Envying	Galatians 5:21
O.	Drunkenness	Galatians 5:21
P.	Reveling	Galatians 5:21
Q.	And such like	Galatians 5:21

What is it that defiles a man?

Mark 18-22

And he saith unto them, Are ye so without understanding also? Do ye not perceive, that whatsoever thing from without entereth into the man, it cannot defile him; 19 Because it entereth not into his heart, but into the belly, and goeth out into the draught, purging all meats? 20 And he said, That which cometh out of the man, that defileth the man. 21 For from within, out of the heart of men, proceed evil thoughts, adulteries, fornications, murders, 22 Thefts, covetousness, wickedness, deceit, lasciviousness, an evil eye, blasphemy, pride, foolishness: 23 All these evil things come from within, and defile the man.

Remember what God did because of the wickedness of Man

Genesis 6:1-22

And it came to pass, when men began to multiply on the face of the earth, and daughters were born unto them, 2 That the sons of God saw the daughters of men that they were fair; and they took them wives of all which they chose. 3 And the LORD said, My spirit shall not always strive with man, for that he also is flesh: yet his days shall be an hundred and twenty years. 4 There were giants in the earth in those days; and also after that, when the sons of God came in unto the daughters of men, and they bare children to them, the same became mighty men which were of old, men of renown. 5 And God saw that the wickedness of man was great in the earth, and that every imagination of the thoughts of his heart was only evil continually. 6 And it repented the LORD that he had made man on the earth, and it grieved him at his heart. 7 And the LORD said, I will destroy man whom I have created from the face of the earth; both man, and beast, and the creeping thing, and the fowls of the air; for it repenteth me that I have made them. 8 But Noah found grace in the eyes of the LORD. 9 These are the generations of Noah: Noah was a just man and perfect in his generations, and Noah walked with God. 10 And Noah begat three sons, Shem, Ham, and Japheth. 11 The earth also was corrupt before God, and the earth was filled with violence. 12 And God looked upon the earth, and, behold, it was corrupt; for all flesh had corrupted his way upon the earth. 13 And God said unto Noah, The end of all flesh is come before me; for the earth is filled with violence through them; and, behold, I will destroy them with the earth. 14 Make thee an ark of gopher wood; rooms shalt thou make in the ark, and shalt pitch it within and without with pitch. 15 And this is the fashion which thou shalt make it of: The length of the ark shall be three hundred cubits, the breadth of it fifty cubits, and the height of it thirty cubits. 16 A window shalt thou make to the ark, and in a cubit shalt thou finish it above; and the door of the ark shalt thou set in the side thereof; with lower, second, and third stories shalt thou make it. 17 And, behold, I, even I, do bring a flood of waters upon the earth, to destroy all flesh, wherein is the breath of life, from under heaven; and every thing that is in the earth shall die. 18 But with thee will I establish my covenant; and thou shalt come into the ark, thou, and thy sons, and thy wife, and thy sons' wives with thee. 19 And of every living thing of all flesh, two of every sort shalt thou bring into the ark, to keep them alive with thee; they shall be male and female. 20 Of fowls after their kind, and of cattle after their kind, of every creeping thing of the earth after his kind, two of every sort shall come unto thee, to keep them alive. 21 And take thou unto thee of all food that is eaten, and thou shalt gather it to thee; and it shall be for food for thee, and for them. 22 Thus did Noah; according to all that God commanded him, so did he.

Genesis 9: 11-17
And I will establish my covenant with you; neither shall all flesh be cut off any more by the waters of a flood; neither shall there any more be a flood to destroy the earth. 12 And God said, This is the token of the covenant which I make between me and you and every living creature that is with you, for perpetual generations: 13 I do set my bow in the cloud, and it shall be for a token of a covenant between me and the earth. 14 And it shall come to pass, when I bring a cloud over the earth, that the bow shall be seen in the cloud: 15 And I will remember my covenant, which is between me and you and every living creature of all flesh; and the waters shall no more become a flood to destroy all flesh. 16 And the bow shall be in the

cloud; and I will look upon it, that I may remember the everlasting covenant between God and every living creature of all flesh that is upon the earth. 17 And God said unto Noah, This is the token of the covenant, which I have established between me and all flesh that is upon the earth.

Because of our alienation from God our only hope is in the atonement of Christ. Symbolized in the Old Testament through the sacrificial offering for sin, the atonement found fulfillment in the New Testament. While the atonement is rooted in the nature of God, it was His Grace that made provision for our complete redemption through the death of Christ.

An invitation is given to all; to be saved, live Righteous and Holy.
Matthew 11:28 Come unto me, all ye that labour and are heavy laden and I will give you rest.

John 3:16 For God so loved the world, that he gave his only begotten Son, that whosoever believeth in him should not perish, but have everlasting life.

What did Christ do for us?
Matthew 20:28 Even as the Son of man came not to be ministered unto, but to minister, and to give his life a ransom for many.

1Timothy 2:6 Who gave himself a ransom for all, to be testified in due time.

John 6:51
I am the living bread which came down from heaven: if any man eat of this bread, he shall live for ever: and the bread that I will give is my flesh, which I will give for the life of the world.

Then Jesus said unto them, (v53) Verily, verily, I say unto you, except ye eat the flesh of the Son of man, and drink his blood, ye have no life in you.

Here salvation is available to those who receive it through Christ's death.
Since therefore, we are now justified by His blood, much more shall we be saved by Him from the wrath of God?

Romans 5:9 Much more then, being now justified by his blood, we shall be saved from wrath through him.

What we have in Christ?
Ephesians 1:7 In whom we have redemption through his blood, the forgiveness of sins, according to the riches of his grace;

What we have in Christ?
Colossians 1:14 In whom we have redemption through his blood, even the forgiveness of sins:

What Christ did for us?
1 Peter 1:18-19
Forasmuch as ye know that ye were not redeemed with corruptible things, as silver and gold, from your vain conversation received by tradition from your fathers; But with the precious blood of Christ, as of a lamb without blemish and without spot:

What we need to do!
1 John 1:7 But if we walk in the light, as he is in the light, we have fellowship one with another, and the blood of Jesus Christ his Son cleanseth us from all sin.

The Believers was washed!
Revelation 7:14 And I said unto him, Sir, thou knowest. And he said to me, these are they which came out of great tribulation, and

have washed their robes, and made them white in the blood of the Lamb.

What Christ did for us?
Revelation 1:5
And from Jesus Christ, who is the faithful witness, and the first begotten of the dead, and the prince of the kings of the earth. Unto him that loved us, and washed us from our sins in his own blood,

What Christ did for us?
Revelation 5:9 "Thou wast slain, and hast redeemed us to God by thy blood out of every kindred, and tongue, and people, and nation."

Upon these scriptural bases we behold God's plan for our salvation. The call of Christ to redemption is given freely to everyone. *"Come unto me, all ye that labour and are heavy laden, and I will give you rest." –Matthew 11:28.* However, our free moral choice must be considered in accepting or rejecting "so great of salvation." The call is universally extended but the decision is with the individual person.

There are several things that must be produced in us by the Holy Spirit. (1) A conviction, (2) Recognize a need of salvation (3) Godly sorrow (4) Repentance (5) Confession (6) Forgiveness.

(1) **Conviction:** Produced by the Holy Spirit through the Word of God, referred to as a spiritual awakening.

(2) **Having recognized the need for salvation,** individuals who are aware of this guilt weighing upon their souls must have a wiliness to meet the conditions of the Bible.

(3) **Godly sorrow** reveals the desire of the unsaved to be forgiven. It is an inward awareness that without God's forgiveness we are eternally lost. It is a deep sense of regret for the wrongs committed.

2 Corinthians 7:10 For godly sorrow worketh repentance to salvation not to be repented of: but the sorrow of the world worketh death

(4) **Repentance:** When one desires to be saved, it is determined by the individual's willingness to repent. Repentance is a since of personal guilt of grief for sins committed, hatred toward sin, and a determined turning away from it. Foremost in our understanding of repentance is that of forsaking sin.

Acts 3:19 Repent ye therefore, and be converted, that your sins may be blotted out, when the times of refreshing shall come from the presence of the Lord.

Psalm 51:17 The sacrifices of God are a broken spirit: a broken and a contrite heart, O God, thou wilt not despise.

(5) **Confession:** Most difficult for some, is the act of confession. With out this openness with God and us there can be no real peace.

Romans 10:9-10
That if thou shalt confess with thy mouth the Lord Jesus, and shalt believe in thine heart that God hath raised him from the dead, thou shalt be saved. For with the heart man believeth unto righteousness; and with the mouth confession is made unto salvation.

Proverbs 28:13 He that covereth his sins shall not prosper: but whoso confesseth and forsaketh them shall have mercy.

1John 1:9 informs us that the confession must be made unto the Lord. *"If we say that we have no sin, we deceive ourselves, and the truth is not in us."*

But it is also essential that we effect reconciliation with others as we confess to people we may have wronged.

Acts 24:16 And herein do I exercise myself, to have always a conscience void of offence toward God, and toward men.

Matthew 5:23-24 Therefore if thou bring thy gift to the altar, and there rememberest that thy brother hath ought against thee; Leave there thy gift before the altar, and go thy way; first be reconciled to thy brother, and then come and offer thy gift.

Confession: To God often reveals areas of our lives in which we need to make restitution.

(6) **Forgiveness:** Forgiveness is a two way street. You must forgive others as your Heavenly Father forgives you.

CHAPTER 2

Seven words Jesus used to describe Himself

In John's Gospel Jesus used the phrase "I am"… seven times.
The words: "I am" are solemn and emphatic, for Jesus was describing who he was and what he had come to do.

Exodus 3:14 And God said unto Moses, I AM THAT I AM: and he said, Thus shalt thou say unto the children of Israel, I AM hath sent me unto you.

"I am the bread of life"
John 6:35 And Jesus said unto them, I am the bread of life: he that cometh to me shall never hunger; and he that believeth on me shall never thirst.

"I am that bread of life."
John 6:48 I am that bread of life.

John 6:51 I am the living bread which came down from heaven: if any man eat of this bread, he shall live for ever: and the bread that I will give is my flesh, which I will give for the life of the world.

John 6:41 The Jews then murmured at him, because he said, I am the bread which came down from heaven.

"I am the light of the world"
John 8:12 Then spake Jesus again unto them, saying, I am the light of the world: he that followeth me shall not walk in darkness, but shall have the light of life.

Ovit G. Pursley, Sr.

1John 1:5 This then is the message which we have heard of him, and declare unto you, that God is light, and in him is no darkness at all.

Exodus 13:21 And the LORD went before them by day in a pillar of a cloud, to lead them the way; and by night in a pillar of fire, to give them light; to go by day and night:

Nehemiah 9:12 Moreover thou leddest them in the day by a cloudy pillar; and in the night by a pillar of fire, to give them light in the way wherein they should go.

Matthew 5:14 Ye are the light of the world. A city that is set on an hill cannot be hid.

"I am the door-gate for the sheep"
John 10:7 Then said Jesus unto them again, verily, verily, I say unto you, I am the door of the sheep.

Ezekiel 34:14 I will feed them in a good pasture, and upon the high mountains of Israel shall their fold be: there shall they lie in a good fold, and in a fat pasture shall they feed upon the mountains of Israel.

"I am the good shepherd"
John 10:11 I am the good shepherd: the good shepherd giveth his life for the sheep.

Ezekiel 24:176 Son of man, behold, I take away from thee the desire of thine eyes with a stroke: yet neither shalt thou mourn nor weep, neither shall thy tears run down.

Hebrews 13:20 Now the God of peace, that brought again from the dead our Lord Jesus, that great shepherd of the sheep, through the blood of the everlasting covenant.

I am the resurrection and the life"
John 11:25 Jesus said unto her, I am the resurrection, and the life: he that believeth in me, though he were dead, yet shall he live:

Acts 3:15 And killed the Prince of life, whom God hath raised from the dead; whereof we are witnesses.

Hebrews 7:15 And it is yet far more evident: for that after the similitude of Melchisedec there ariseth another priest.

John 1:4 In him was life; and the life was the light of men.

John 3:15 That whosoever believeth in him should not perish, but have eternal life.

"I am the way and the truth and the life"
John 14:6 Jesus saith unto him, I am the way, the truth, and the life: no man cometh unto the Father, but by me.

Acts 4:12 Neither is there salvation in any other: for there is none other name under heaven given among men, whereby we must be saved.

Hebrews 10:19-20 Having therefore, brethren, boldness to enter into the holiest by the blood of Jesus, 20 By a new and living way, which he hath consecrated for us, through the veil, that is to say, his flesh.

In the early church Christianity was sometimes called "the way"
Acts 19:2 He said unto them, Have ye received the Holy Ghost since ye believed? And they said unto him, We have not so much as heard whether there be any Holy Ghost.

Acts 19:23 And the same time there arose no small stir about that way.

"I am the true vine"
John 15:1 I am the true vine, and my Father is the husbandman.

Jeremiah 2:21 Yet I had planted thee a noble vine, wholly a right seed: how then art thou turned into the degenerate plant of a strange vine unto me?

Isaiah 5:1-7
Now will I sing to my well beloved a song of my beloved touching his vineyard. My wellbeloved hath a vineyard in a very fruitful hill: 2 And he fenced it, and gathered out the stones thereof, and planted it with the choicest vine, and built a tower in the midst of it, and also made a winepress therein: and he looked that it should bring forth grapes, and it brought forth wild grapes. 3 And now, O inhabitants of Jerusalem, and men of Judah, judge, I pray you, betwixt me and my vineyard. 4 What could have been done more to my vineyard that I have not done in it? Wherefore, when I looked that it should bring forth grapes, brought it forth wild grapes? 5 And now go to; I will tell you what I will do to my vineyard: I will take away the hedge thereof, and it shall be eaten up; and break down the wall thereof, and it shall be trodden down: 6 And I will lay it waste: it shall not be pruned, nor digged; but there shall come up briers and thorns: I will also command the clouds that they rain no rain upon it. 7 For the vineyard of the LORD of hosts is the house of Israel, and the men of Judah his pleasant plant: and he looked for judgment, but behold oppression; for righteousness, but behold a cry.

CHAPTER 3

The Birth of Jesus ---
The Ascension

The birth of Jesus
Matt. 1:18-25; See Luke 2:1-20

18 Now the birth of Jesus Christ was on this wise: When as his mother Mary was espoused to Joseph, before they came together, she was found with child of the Holy Ghost. 19 Then Joseph her husband, being a just *man*, and not willing to make her a public example, was minded to put her away privily. 20 But while he thought on these things, behold, the angel of the Lord appeared unto him in a dream, saying, Joseph, thou son of David, fear not to take unto thee Mary thy wife: for that which is conceived in her is of the Holy Ghost. 21 And she shall bring forth a son, and thou shalt call his name JESUS: for he shall save his people from their sins. 22 Now all this was done, that it might be fulfilled which was spoken of the Lord by the prophet, saying, 23 Behold, a virgin shall be with child, and shall bring forth a son, and they shall call his name Emmanuel, which being interpreted is, God with us. 24 Then Joseph being raised from sleep did as the angel of the Lord had bidden him, and took unto him his wife: 25 And knew her not till she had brought forth her firstborn son: and he called his name JESUS.

The Baptism of Jesus
Matthew 3:13-17

Then cometh Jesus from Galilee to Jordan unto John, to be baptized of him. 14 But John forbad him, saying, I have need to be baptized of thee, and comest thou to me? 15 And Jesus answering said unto him, suffer it to be so now: for thus it becometh us to fulfil all righteousness. Then he suffered him. 16 And Jesus, when he was baptized, went up straightway out of the water: and, lo, the heavens were opened unto him, and he saw the Spirit of God descending like a dove, and lighting upon him: 17 And lo a voice from heaven, saying, This is my beloved Son, in whom I am well pleased.

Christ's Early Ministry
Luke 4:16-21
And he came to Nazareth, where he had been brought up: and, as his custom was, he went into the synagogue on the sabbath day, and stood up for to read. 17 And there was delivered unto him the book of the prophet Esaias. And when he had opened the book, he found the place where it was written, 18 The Spirit of the Lord is upon me, because he hath anointed me to preach the gospel to the poor; he hath sent me to heal the brokenhearted, to preach deliverance to the captives, and recovering of sight to the blind, to set at liberty them that are bruised, 19 To preach the acceptable year of the Lord. 20 And he closed the book, and he gave it again to the minister, and sat down. And the eyes of all them that were in the synagogue were fastened on him. 21 And he began to say unto them, this day is this scripture fulfilled in your ears.

Matthew 4:23-25
And Jesus went about all Galilee, teaching in their synagogues, and preaching the gospel of the kingdom, and healing all manner of sickness and all manner of disease among the people. 24 And his fame went throughout all Syria: and they brought unto him all sick people that were taken with divers diseases and torments, and those which were possessed with devils, and those which were lunatic, and those that had the palsy; and he healed them. 25 And there followed him great multitudes of people from Galilee, and from Decapolis, and from Jerusalem, and from Judaea, and from beyond Jordan.

Christ's Public Offer of Himself as King
The Triumphant Entry

Matthew 21: 1-11
And when they drew nigh unto Jerusalem, and were come to Bethphage, unto the mount of Olives, then sent Jesus two disciples,

2 Saying unto them, Go into the village over against you, and straightway ye shall find an ass tied, and a colt with her: loose them, and bring them unto me. 3 And if any man say ought unto you, ye shall say, The Lord hath need of them; and straightway he will send them. 4 All this was done, that it might be fulfilled which was spoken by the prophet, saying, 5 Tell ye the daughter of Sion, Behold, thy King cometh unto thee, meek, and sitting upon an ass, and a colt the foal of an ass. 6 And the disciples went, and did as Jesus commanded them, 7 And brought the ass, and the colt, and put on them their clothes, and they set him thereon. 8 And a very great multitude spread their garments in the way; others cut down branches from the trees, and strowed them in the way. 9 And the multitudes that went before, and that followed, cried, saying, Hosanna to the son of David: Blessed is he that cometh in the name of the Lord; Hosanna in the highest. 10 And when he was come into Jerusalem, all the city was moved, saying, Who is this? 11 And the multitude said, This is Jesus the prophet of Nazareth of Galilee.

Betrayal and Arrest
Matthew 26:3-4
Then assembled together the chief priests, and the scribes, and the elders of the people, unto the palace of the high priest, who was called Caiaphas, 4 And consulted that they might take Jesus by subtlety, and kill him.

Mark 14:10-11 And Judas Iscariot, one of the twelve, went unto the chief priests, to betray him unto them. 11 And when they heard it, they were glad, and promised to give him money. And he sought how he might conveniently betray him.

Mark 14:32-46
And they came to a place which was named Gethsemane: and he saith to his disciples, Sit ye here, while I shall pray. 33 And he taketh with him Peter and James and John, and began to be sore amazed, and to be very heavy; 34 And saith unto them, My soul is exceeding sorrowful unto death: tarry ye here, and watch. 35 And

he went forward a little, and fell on the ground, and prayed that, if it were possible, the hour might pass from him. 36 And he said, Abba, Father, all things are possible unto thee; take away this cup from me: nevertheless not what I will, but what thou wilt. 37 And he cometh, and findeth them sleeping, and saith unto Peter, Simon, sleepest thou? Couldest not thou watch one hour? 38 Watch ye and pray, lest ye enter into temptation. The spirit truly is ready, but the flesh is weak. 39 And again he went away, and prayed, and spake the same words. 40 And when he returned, he found them asleep again, (for their eyes were heavy,) neither wist they what to answer him. 41 And he cometh the third time, and saith unto them, Sleep on now, and take your rest: it is enough, the hour is come; behold, the Son of man is betrayed into the hands of sinners. 42 Rise up, let us go; lo, he that betrayeth me is at hand. 43 And immediately, while he yet spake, cometh Judas, one of the twelve, and with him a great multitude with swords and staves, from the chief priests and the scribes and the elders. 44 And he that betrayed him had given them a token, saying, Whomsoever I shall kiss, that same is he; take him, and lead him away safely. 45 And as soon as he was come, he goeth straightway to him, and saith, Master, master; and kissed him. 46 And they laid their hands on him, and took him.

Matthew 26:47-49
And while he yet spake, lo, Judas, one of the twelve, came, and with him a great multitude with swords and staves, from the chief priests and elders of the people. 48 Now he that betrayed him gave them a sign, saying, Whomsoever I shall kiss, that same is he: hold him fast. 49 And forthwith he came to Jesus, and said, Hail, master; and kissed him.
Matthew 27:1-2
When the morning was come, all the chief priests and elders of the people took counsel against Jesus to put him to death: 2 And when they had bound him, they led him away, and delivered him to Pontius Pilate the governor.
Luke 23:14 I having examine before you, have found no fault in this man teaching those those things whereof ye accuse him.

Luke 23:23:24 And they were instant with loud voices, requiring that he might be crucified. And the voices of them and of the chief priests prevailed. 24 And Pilate gave sentence that it should be as they required.

The Crucifixion
Matthew 27:27-31
Then the soldiers of the governor took Jesus into the common hall, and gathered unto him the whole band of soldiers. 28 And they stripped him, and put on him a scarlet robe. 29 And when they had platted a crown of thorns, they put it upon his head, and a reed in his right hand: and they bowed the knee before him, and mocked him, saying, Hail, King of the Jews! 30 And they spit upon him, and took the reed, and smote him on the head. 31 And after that they had mocked him, they took the robe off from him, and put his own raiment on him, and led him away to crucify him.

Matthew 27: 46 And about the ninth hour Jesus cried with a loud voice, saying, Eli, Eli, lama sabachthani? That is to say, My God, my God, why hast thou forsaken me?

Matthew 27:50 Jesus, when he had cried again with a loud voice, yielded up the ghost.

Matthew 27:57-60
When the even was come, there came a rich man of Arimathaea, named Joseph, who also himself was Jesus' disciple: 58 He went to Pilate, and begged the body of Jesus. Then Pilate commanded the body to be delivered. 59 And when Joseph had taken the body, he wrapped it in a clean linen cloth, 60 And laid it in his own new tomb, which he had hewn out in the rock: and he rolled a great stone to the door of the sepulchre, and departed.

Ovit G. Pursley, Sr.

The Resurrection
Matthew 28:1-7

In the end of the sabbath, as it began to dawn toward the first day of the week, came Mary Magdalene and the other Mary to see the sepulchre.2 And, behold, there was a great earthquake: for the angel of the Lord descended from heaven, and came and rolled back the stone from the door, and sat upon it. 3 His countenance was like lightning, and his raiment white as snow: 4 And for fear of him the keepers did shake, and became as dead men. 5 And the angel answered and said unto the women, Fear not ye: for I know that ye seek Jesus, which was crucified. 6 He is not here: for he is risen, as he said. Come, see the place where the Lord lay. 7 And go quickly, and tell his disciples that he is risen from the dead; and, behold, he goeth before you into Galilee; there shall ye see him: lo, I have told you.

The Ascension
Acts 1:4, 8-9

And, being assembled together with them, commanded them that they should not depart from Jerusalem, but wait for the promise of the Father, which, saith he, ye have heard of me …But ye shall receive power, after that the Holy Ghost is come upon you: and ye shall be witnesses unto me both in Jerusalem, and in all Judaea, and in Samaria, and unto the uttermost part of the earth. And when he had spoken these things, while they beheld, he was taken up; and a cloud received him out of their sight.

CHAPTER 4

What Must I Do To Be Saved?

The Bible can give us all the answers we need.
What did God do for our Salvation?

John 3:16

For God so loved the world, that he gave his only begotten Son, that whosoever believeth in him should not perish, but have everlasting life.

The reason we need Salvation is because of our alienation from God. Therefore our only hope is in the atonement of Jesus Christ. Symbolized in the Old Testament through the sacrificial offering for sin, the atonement is rooted in the nature of God. It was His Grace that made provision for our complete redemption through the death of Christ.

Eccl 7:20

For *there is* not a just man upon earth, that doeth good, and sinneth not.

Rom 3:23

For all have sinned, and come short of the glory of God;

Rom 6:23

For the wages of sin *is* death; but the gift of God is eternal life through Jesus Christ our Lord.

So as believers, the first thing we need to know is what Christ **did for us** and what **we have in** Christ. First let us see *what Christ did for* us. Matthew. 20:28 says, "The son of man came...to give His life for a ransom for many."

1 Tim. 2:6 says, "Who gave His life as a ransom for all."

1 Peter 1:18-19 says, "You were ransom from the futile ways inherited from your fathers, not with perishable things such as silver and gold but with the precious blood of Christ, like that of a lamb without blemish or spot."

Rev. 1:5 says, "To him who loved us, and freed us from our sins by His blood."
Rev. 5:9 says, "Thou was slain and by thy blood did ransom men for God."
Secondly, *what we have in Christ.*
Eph. 1:7 says, "In Him we have redemption through His blood, the forgiveness of our trespasses."
Col. 1:14 says, "In whom we have redemption, the forgiveness of sins."
Rev. 7:14 says "They have washed their robes and made them white in the blood of the lamb."

We come to know Jesus in many ways.
First, by the Word of God.
He is the living Word of God
The Son of God
The coming Messiah
Jesus Christ the anointed one
The Savior
The one who gives eternal life
As the way, the truth, and the life
Healer and deliverer
As the one who baptizes with the Holy Ghost
As the only Name whereby we can be saved
Alfa and Omega

We also know Jesus as:
The only way to the Father
The only way to salvation
The only way to truth
The only way to peace

The only way to Heaven
The only way to eternal life

We have come to know Jesus by these and many other names and ways according to the Word of God. We see His as Conqueror, Warrior, and King of Kings and Lord of Lords. Truly fulfilling the words, after His resurrection...wherein He said: *"all power is given unto me in heaven and in earth."* So the question is; how did Jesus get His name with so much authority? The answer is found in three different scriptures:

How Jesus obtained His Name
Phil. 2:9-11 (By bestowal)
Wherefore God also hath highly exalted him, and given him a name which is above every name: [10]That at the name of Jesus every knee should bow, of *things* in heaven, and *things* in earth, and *things* under the earth; [11]And *that* every tongue should confess that Jesus Christ *is* Lord, to the glory of God the Father.
Heb. 1:4-5 (By inheritance)
Being made so much better than the angels, as he hath by inheritance obtained a more excellent name than they. [5]For unto which of the angels said he at any time, Thou art my Son, this day have I begotten thee? And again, I will be to him a Father, and he shall be to me a Son?

Col. 2:15: (By conquest)
And having spoiled principalities and powers, he made a show of them openly, triumphing over them in it.

Therefore, having this knowledge, we are admonished to do several things according to the scriptures.
1. Put on the whole armor of God.-Ephesians 6:11
2. Put on the armor of light.-Romans 13:12
3. Be diligent.-2 Peter 3:14
4. Be steadfast, unmovable.-1 Corinthians 15:58

5. Always abound in the work of the Lord. - 1Corinthians 15:8
6. Work while it is day. -John 9:4
7. Pray without ceasing. -1Thes. 5:17
8. Be ye separate says the Lord and touch not the unclean thing and I will receive you. -2 Corinthians 6:17

What we need to do!

1 John 1:7 says, "But if we walk in the light, as he is in the light, we have fellowship with one another, and the blood of Jesus his Son cleanses us from all sin."

Key: Your duty as a born again believer is to say the same thing that God says according to His Word. You may not understand it, but it will give the Word and the Spirit free course to accomplish that which pleases the Heavenly Father and the Lord Jesus Christ. Hebrews 4:12 says: *"For the word of God is quick, and powerful, and sharper than any twoedged sword, piercing even to the dividing asunder of soul and spirit, and of the joints and marrow, and is a discerner of the thoughts and intents of the heart."* According to Hebrews 4:12, the power and ability of God is in His Word.

I want to list a few scriptures that show what *you* must do to be born again, that is, to obtain *salvation and Eternal life.*

Salvation and life (New Birth-Born Again)
John 3:16
16For God so loved the world, that he gave his only begotten Son, that whosoever believeth in him should not perish, but have everlasting life.

John 6:40
And this is the will of him that sent me, that every one which seeth the Son, and believeth on him, may have everlasting life: and I will raise him up at the last day.

Acts 2:38-39
Then Peter said unto them, Repent, and be baptized every one of you in the name of Jesus Christ for the remission of sins, and ye shall receive the gift of the Holy Ghost. [39] For the promise is unto you, and to your children, and to all that are afar off, *even* as many as the Lord our God shall call.

Acts 17:30 And the times of this ignorance God winked at; but now commandeth all men every where to repent:

Luke 13:3 I tell you, Nay: but, except ye repent, ye shall all likewise perish.

2 Cor 7:10
For godly sorrow worketh repentance to salvation not to be repented of but the sorrow of the world worketh death.

John 5:24
Verily, verily, I say unto you, He that heareth my word, and believeth on him that sent me, hath everlasting life, and shall not come into condemnation; but is passed from death unto life.

1 John 5:1
Whosoever believeth that Jesus is the Christ is born of God: and every one that loveth him that begat loveth him also that is begotten of him.

Mark 16:15-16
And he said unto them, Go ye into all the world, and preach the gospel to every creature. [16]He that believeth and is baptized shall be saved; but he that believeth not shall be damned.

Acts 16:30-31
And brought them out, and said, Sirs, what must I do to be saved? [31]And they said, Believe on the Lord Jesus Christ, and thou shalt be saved, and thy house.

The evidence is in; the scriptures just mention is overwhelming clear about what the Bible teaches about *salvation and life*. In these and other scripture references you will find words like, "believe," "repent," "confess," "be baptized," call on the name of Jesus," and according to Acts 16:31; *"Believe on the Lord Jesus Christ, and thou shalt be saved. And thy house. "*

My friend: that's what it takes to be saved! These scriptures teach us what *you* must do in order to have salvation, eternal life, everlasting life, born again, and the new birth. They are talking about the regeneration work of the Holy Spirit

Salvation and Assurance
Upon these scriptural bases we behold God's plan for our salvation. However, our free moral choice must be considered in accepting or rejecting "so great of salvation." The call of Christ to redemption is given freely to everyone. *"Come to me all who labor and are heavy laden, and I will give you rest." (Matt. 11:28).* The invitation is universally extended but the decision is with the individual person.

First, there must be a conviction!
(1) **Conviction...**produced by the Holy Spirit through the Word of God...refereed to as the spiritual awakening.
(2) Having **recognized the need for salvation**, individuals who are aware of guilt weighing upon their souls must desire to be saved (Acts 16:30). There must be a willingness to meet the conditions of the Bible, the word of God.
(3) **Godly** sorrow...reveals the desire of the unsaved to be forgiven. It is an inward awareness that without God's forgiveness we are eternally lost. It is a deep sense of regret for the wrongs committed. 2 Corinthians. 7:10 says, *"For godly grief produces a repentance that leads to salvation and brings no regret, but worldly grief produces death."*
(4) **Desire to be saved**...when one desire to be saved, it is determined by the individuals willingness to repent. Repentance is a sense

of personal grief for sins committed, hatred toward sin, and a determined turning from it. (Acts 3:19; Isaiah. 55:7)

(5) **Confession...**confession is most difficult for some. Without this openness with God and our selves there can be no peace.

Proverbs 28:13
He who conceals his transgressions will not prosper, but he who confess and forsake them will obtain mercy.

Confession is to be made to the Lord.
1 John 1:9 *"If we confess our sins, he is faithful and just, and will forgive our sins."* But it is also essential, that we effect reconciliation with others as we confess to people we have wronged. (Acts 24:16; Matt.5:23-24)

Confession to God often reveals areas of our lives in which we need to make restitution. Therefore, forgiveness is a two way street, allowing the Holy Spirit to bring conviction.
Salvation is Gods gift to the believer. However, our continuing walk with the Lord is dependent upon our obedience to His word.
Evidence (Results) of salvation
Love of the Brethren.
1 John 3:14
We know that we have passed from death unto life, because we love the brethren. He that loveth not his brother abideth in death.

The witness of the Holy Spirit.
1 John 5:10
He that believeth on the Son of God hath the witness in himself: he that believeth not God hath made him a liar; because he believeth not the record that God gave of his Son.

Rom. 8:16 The Spirit itself beareth witness with our spirit, that we are the children of God:

The leading of the Spirit.

Rom 8:14

For as many as are led by the Spirit of God, they are the sons of God.

The Love of God shed abroad in the heart by the Holy Spirit.

Rom. 5:5

And hope maketh not ashamed; because the love of God is shed abroad in our hearts by the Holy Ghost which is given unto us.

The fruit of the Spirit.

Gal. 5:22

But the fruit of the Spirit is love, joy, peace, longsuffering, gentleness, goodness, faith.

Keeping the commandments of Christ.

1 John 2:3-6

And hereby we do know that we know him, if we keep his commandments. 4 He that saith, I know him, and keepeth not his commandments, is a liar, and the truth is not in him. 5 But whoso keepeth his word, in him verily is the love of God perfected: hereby know we that we are in him. 6 He that saith he abideth in him ought himself also so to walk, even as he walked.

1 John 3:23-24

And this is his commandment, That we should believe on the name of his Son Jesus Christ, and love one another, as he gave us commandment. 24 And he that keepeth his commandments dwelleth in him, and he in him. And hereby we know that he abideth in us, by the Spirit which he hath given us.

Doing righteousness.
1 John 3:10
In this the children of God are manifest, and the children of the devil: whosoever doeth not righteousness is not of God, neither he that loveth not his brother.

Overcoming the world.
1 John 2:15
Love not the world, neither the things that are in the world. If any man love the world, the love of the Father is not in him.

1 John 5:14
And this is the confidence that we have in him, that, if we ask any thing according to his will, he heareth us.

Willingness to confess Christ publicly.
Rom. 10:9
That if thou shalt confess with thy mouth the Lord Jesus, and shalt believe in thine heart that God hath raised him from the dead, thou shalt be saved.

Matt. 10:32-33
Whosoever therefore shall confess me before men, him will I confess also before my Father which is in heaven. 33 But whosoever shall deny me before men, him will I also deny before my Father which is in heaven.

1 John 4:2
Hereby know ye the Spirit of God: Every Spirit that confesseth that Jesus is cometh in the flesh is of God.

Spiritual understanding
1 John 2:20-26
But ye have an unction from the Holy One, and ye know all things. 21 I have not written unto you because ye know not the truth, but because ye know it, and that no lie is of the truth. 22 Who is a liar

but he that denieth that Jesus is the Christ? He is antichrist, that denieth the Father and the Son.23 Whosoever denotes the Son, the same hath not the Father: (but) he that acknowledgeth the Son hath the Father also. 24 Let that therefore abide in you, which ye have heard from the beginning. If that which ye have heard from the beginning shall remain in you, ye also shall continue in the Son, and in the Father. 25 And this is the promise that he hath promised us, even eternal life. 26 These things have I written unto you concerning them that seduce you.

1 John 5:20
And we know that the Son of God is come, and hath given us an understanding, that we may know him that is true, and we are in him that is true, even in his Son Jesus Christ. This is the true God, and eternal life.

1 Cor. 2:12-15
Now we have received, not the spirit of the world, but the spirit which is of God; that we might know the things that are freely given to us of God. 13 Which things also we speak, not in the words which man's wisdom teacheth, but which the Holy Ghost teacheth; comparing spiritual things with spiritual. 14 But the natural man receiveth not the things of the Spirit of God: for they are foolishness unto him: neither can he know them, because they are spiritually discerned. 15 But he that is spiritual judgeth all things, yet he himself is judged of no man.

2 Pet 3:9
The Lord is not slack concerning his promise, as some men count slackness; but is longsuffering to us-ward, not willing that any **should perish,** but that all should come to **repentance.**

What does the Bible say about the ability of God's word?
Heb 4:12
For the word of God *is* quick, and powerful, and sharper than any twoedged sword, piercing even to the dividing asunder of soul

and spirit, and of the joints and marrow, and *is a* discerner of the thoughts and intents of the heart.

What is the Word of God good for?
2 Tim 3:16

All scripture *is* given by inspiration of God, and *is* profitable for doctrine, for reproof, for correction, for instruction in righteousness:

What has the Lord given unto man in His word?
2 Pet 1:3

According as his divine power hath given unto us all things that *pertain* unto life and godliness, through the knowledge of him that hath called us to glory and virtue:

What did God say about His word?
Ezek 12:25

For I *am* the LORD: I will speak, and the word that I shall speak shall come to pass; it shall be no more pronged: for in your days, 0 rebellious house, will I say the word, and will perform it, saith the Lord GOD.

What did Jesus say about His word?
Mat 24:35

Heaven and earth shall pass away, but my words shall not pass away.

How long has the Word of God been around?
John 1:1-5

In the beginning was the Word, and the Word was with God, and the Word was God. ² The same was in the beginning with God. All things were made by him; and without him was not any thing made that was made. ⁴ In him was life; and the life was the light of men. ⁵ And the light shineth in darkness; and the darkness comprehended it not.

Jesus is the true light that came into the world that we might believe on His Name.

John 1:6-12

There was a man sent from God, whose name *was* John. The same came for a witness, to bear witness of the Light, that all *men* through him might believe. [5] He was not that Light, but *was sent* to bear witness of that Light. [9] *That* was the true Light, which lighteth every man that cometh into the world. [10] He was in the world, and the world was made by him, and the world knew him not. [11] He came unto his own, and his own received him not. [12] But as many as received him, to them gave he power to become the sons of God, *even* to them that believe on his name:

Remember how Jesus obtained His name.

This is what set Jesus apart from any other person. *God exalted Him; given Him a name above every name; that at the name of Jesus every knee should bow, of things in heaven, and things in earth, and things under the earth.*

There are three ways in which Jesus obtains His name:

(1) **Bestowal**

Phil 2:9-11

Wherefore God also hath highly exalted him, and given him a name which is above every name: [10] That at the name of Jesus every knee should bow, of *things* in heaven, and *things* in earth, and *things* under the earth; [11] And *that* every tongue should confess that Jesus Christ *is* Lord, to the glory of God the Father.

(2) **Inheritance**

Heb 1:4-5

Being made so much better than the angels, as he hath by inheritance obtained a more excellent name than they. [5] For unto which of the angels said he at any time, Thou art my Son, this day have I begotten thee? And again, I will be to him a Father, and he shall be to me a Son?

(3) **Conquest**

Col 2:15 *And* having spoiled principalities and powers, he made a show of them openly, triumphing over them in it.

Then Jesus gave the church (the saints) the authority in His name.

John 16:24

Hitherto have ye asked nothing in my name: ask, and ye shall receive, that your joy may be full.

CHAPTER 5

What Must I Do To Be Saved?

God So Loved the World
John 3:16
For God so loved the world, that he gave his only begotten Son, that whosoever believeth in him should not perish, but have everlasting life.

Man is a sinner and sin has separated him from God.
Eccl 7:20
For *there is* not a just man upon earth, that doeth good, and sinneth not.

Rom 3:23
For all have sinned, and come short of the glory of God;

The wages of sin is death.
Rom 6:23
For the wages of sin is death; but the gift of God *is* eternal life through Jesus Christ our Lord.

Jesus Christ is the only remedy for sin.
1 Pet 3:18
Neither is there salvation in any other: for there is none other name under heaven given among men, whereby we must be saved.

You must receive Jesus Christ as your personal Lord and Savior.
Mat 28:19-20
Go ye therefore, and teach all nations, baptizing them in the name of the Father, and of the Son, and of the Holy Ghost: [20] Teaching them

to observe all things whatsoever I have commanded you: and, lo, I am with you alway, *even* unto the end of the world. Amen.

Believe and be baptized.
Mark 16:15-16
And he said unto them, Go ye into all the world, and preach the gospel to every creature. [16] He that believeth and is baptized shall be saved; but he that believeth not shall be damned.

Confess with your mouth.
Rom 10:9
That if thou shalt confess with thy mouth the Lord Jesus, and shalt believe in thine heart that God hath raised him from the dead, thou shalt be saved.

It must start in your heart-spirit and then get in your mouth.
Rom 10:10
For with the heart man believeth unto righteousness; and with the mouth confession is made unto salvation.

You shall not be ashamed.
Rom 10:11-12
For the scripture saith, whosoever believeth on him shall not be ashamed. [12] For there is no difference between the Jew and the Greek: for the same Lord over all is rich unto all that call upon him.

Call upon the name of the Lord and thou shall be saved.
Rom 10:13-15
For whosoever shall call upon the name of the Lord shall be saved. [14] How then shall they call on him in whom they have not believed? And how shall they believe in him of whom they have not heard? And how shall they hear without a preacher? is And how shall they preach, except they be sent? As it is written, how beautiful are the feet of them that preach the gospel of peace, and bring glad tidings of good things!

Ovit G. Pursley, Sr.

(1) **"How then shall they call on Him in whom they have not believed?"**

Answer: "The lost (sinner) cannot call upon Him until they believe."

1 Cor 15:1-4

Moreover, brethren, I declare unto you the gospel which I preached unto you, which also ye have received, and wherein ye stand; ² By which also ye are saved, if ye keep in memory what I preached unto you, unless ye have believed in vain. 3For I delivered unto you first of all that which I also received, how that Christ died for our sins according to the scriptures; 4And that he was buried, and that he rose again the third day according to the scriptures:

(2) **"How shall they believe in Him of whom they have not heard?"**

Answer: The lost (sinner) cannot believe in Him until they hear the good news of salvation."

A. The eunuch had to hear to believe.

Acts 8:26-28

And the angel of the Lord spake unto Philip, saying, Arise, and go toward the south unto the way that goeth down from Jerusalem unto Gaza, which is desert. ²⁷ And he arose and went: and, behold, a man of Ethiopia, an eunuch of great authority under Candace queen of the Ethiopians, who had the charge of all her treasure, and had come to Jerusalem for to worship, ²⁸ Was returning, and sitting in his chariot read Esaias the prophet.

Acts 8:29-33

₂₉ Then the Spirit said unto Philip, Go near, and join thyself to this chariot. ³⁰ And Philip ran thither to *him,* and heard him read the prophet Esaias, and said, Understandest thou what thou readest? ³¹ And he said, How can I, except some man should guide me? And he desired Philip that he would come up and sit with him. ³² The place of the scripture which he read was this, He was led as a sheep to the slaughter; and like a lamb dumb before his shearer, so opened he not his mouth: ³³ In his humiliation his judgment was taken away: and who shall declare his generation? For his life is taken from the earth.

Acts 8:34-37
34 And the eunuch answered Philip, and said, I pray thee, of whom speaketh the prophet this? of himself, or of some other man? ³⁵ Then Philip opened his mouth, and began at the same scripture, and preached unto him Jesus. ³⁶ And as they went on *their* way, they came unto a certain water: and the eunuch said, See, *here is* water; what doth hinder me to be baptized? ³⁷ And Philip said, If thou believest with all thine heart, thou mayest. And he answered and said, I believe that Jesus Christ is the Son of God.

Acts 8:38-39
And he commanded the chariot to stand still: and they went down both into the water, both Philip and the eunuch; and he baptized him. 39 And when they were come up out of the water, the Spirit of the Lord caught away Philip, that the eunuch saw him no more: and he went on his way rejoicing.

B. Paul had to hear to believe.
Acts 9:1-6
And Saul, yet breathing out threatenings and slaughter against the disciples of the Lord, went unto the high priest,² And desired of him letters to Damascus to the synagogues, that if he found any of this way, whether they were men or women, he might bring them bound unto Jerusalem. ³ And as he journeyed, he came near Damascus: and suddenly there shines round about him a light from heaven: ⁴ And he fell to the earth and heard a voice saying unto him, Saul, Saul, why persecutes thou me? ⁵ And he said, Who art thou, Lord? And the Lord said, I am Jesus whom thou persecutest: *it is* hard for thee to kick against the pricks. ⁶ And he trembling and astonished said Lord, what wilt thou have me to do? And the Lord *said* unto him, Arise, and go into the city, and it shall be told thee what thou must do.

Acts 9:7-9

And the men which journeyed with him stood speechless hearing a voice, but seeing no man. [8] And Saul arose from the earth; and when his eyes were opened, he saw no man: but the: led him by the hand, and brought *him* into Damascus. [9] And he was three days without sight, and neither did eat nor drink.

Acts 9:10-16

And there was a certain disciple at Damascus, names Ananias; and to him said the Lord in a vision, Ananias. And he said, Behold, I *am here,* Lord. 11 And the Lord *said* unto him Arise, and go into the street which is called Straight, and inquire in the house of Judas for *one* called Saul, of Tarsus: for behold, he prayeth, [12] And hath seen in a vision a man name Ananias coming in, and putting *his* hand on him, that he might receive his sight. [13] Then Ananias answered, Lord, I have heard by many of this man, how much evil he hath done to thy saint at Jerusalem: [14] And here he hath authority from the chief priests to bind all that call on thy name. [15] But the Lord said unto him, Go thy way: for he is a chosen vessel unto me, to bear my name before the Gentiles, and kings, and the children of Israel: [16] For I will show him how great things he must suffer for my name's sake.

Acts 9:17-18

And Ananias went his way, and entered into the house; and putting his hands on him said, Brother Saul, the Lord, *even* Jesus, that appeared unto thee in the way as thou camest, hath sent me, that thou mightest receive thy sight, and be filled with the Holy Ghost. [18] And immediately there fell from his eyes as it had been scales: and he received sight forthwith, and arose, and was baptized.

C. Cornelius had to hear to believe

Acts 10:1-6

There was a certain man in Caesarea called Cornelius, a centurion of the band called the Italian *band, 2 A* devout *man,* and one that feared God with all his house, which gave much alms to the

people, and prayed to God alway. ³ He saw in a vision evidently about the ninth hour of the day an angel of God coming in to him, and saying unto him, Cornelius.⁴ And when he looked on him, he was afraid, and said, What is it, Lord? And he said unto him, Thy prayers and thine alms are come up for a memorial before God. ⁵ And now send men to Joppa, and call for *one* Simon, whose surname is Peter: ⁶ He lodgeth with one
 Simon a tanner, whose house is by the sea side: he shall tell thee what thou oughtest to do.

Acts 10:30-33
And Cornelius said, Four days ago I was fasting until this hour; and at the ninth hour I prayed in my house, and, behold, a man stood before me in bright clothing, ³¹ And said, Cornelius, thy prayer is heard, and thine alms are had in remembrance in the sight of God. ³² Send therefore to Joppa and call hither Simon, whose surname is Peter; he is lodged it the house of *one* Simon a tanner by the sea side: who, when he cometh, shall speak unto thee. ³³ Immediately therefore I sent to thee; and thou hast well done that thou art come. Nov therefore are we all here present before God, to hear all thing: that are commanded thee of God.

Acts 10:34-43
Then Peter opened *his* mouth, and said, Of a truth I perceive that God is no respecter of persons: ³⁵ But in every nation he that feareth him, and worketh righteousness, is accepted with him. ³⁶ The word which *God* sent unto the children of Israel preaching peace by Jesus Christ: (he is Lord of all:) ³⁷ That word, *I say,* ye know, which was published throughout al Judaea, and began from Galilee, after the baptism which John preached; ³⁸ How God anointed Jesus of Nazareth with the Holy Ghost and with power: who went about doing good, and healing all that were oppressed of the devil; for God was with him. ³⁹ And we are witnesses of all things which he did both it the land of the Jews, and in Jerusalem; whom they slew and hanged on a tree: ⁴⁰ Him God raised up the third day, and showed him openly; ⁴¹ Not to all the people, but unto witnesse, chosen before of God,

even to us, who did eat and drink with him after he rose from the dead. [42] And he commanded us to preach unto the people, and to testify that it is he which was, ordained of God *to be* the Judge of quick and dead. [43] To him give all the prophets witness, that through his name whosoever believeth in him shall receive remission of sins.

Acts 10:44-48
While Peter yet spake these words, the Holy Ghost fell on all them which heard the word. [45] And they of the circumcision which believed were astonished, as many as came with Peter because that on the Gentiles also was poured out the gift of the Holy Ghost. [46] For they heard them speak with tongues, and magnify God. Then answered Peter, [47] Can any man forbid water, that these should not be baptized, which have received the Holy Ghost as well as we? [48] And he commanded them to be baptized in the name of the Lord. Then prayed they him to tarry certain days.

"How can they hear without a witness?"
Answer: They cannot hear the news of salvation without a witness.

For example:
1. Three thousand was saved on the day of Pentecost because the 120 both men and women witness.
2. The eunuch was saved because Philip witness.
3. Paul was saved because Ananias witness.
4. Cornelius and his house was saved because Peter witness.
5. The Samaritans was saved because Philip witness.
6. The Philippians' jailer and his house were saved because Paul and Silas witness.
7. All saints was saved because someone preached (witness) to them   about Jesus Christ and the   good news of salvation.

1 John 5:1
Whosoever believeth that Jesus is the Christ is born of God: and every one that loveth him that begat loveth him also that is begotten of him.

John 3:3
Jesus answered and said unto him, Verily, verily, I say unto thee, except a man be born again, he cannot see the kingdom of God. [Jesus calls receiving Him as Lord and Savior the New Birth.]

CHAPTER 6

What Must I Do To Be Saved?

Some say, I am a good man or good woman; I do good things. I do not steal, kill, commit fornication, or adultery. Therefore I do not think I will be lost if I die, even though I do not go to church.

What does the Word of God say about it?
Titus 3:5
Not by works of righteousness which we have done, but according to his mercy he saved us, by the washing of regeneration, and renewing of the Holy Ghost;

Romans3:9-18
What then? are we better *than they?* No, in no wise: for we have before proved both Jews and Gentiles that they are all under sin; ¹⁰ As it is written, There is none righteous, no, not one: ¹¹ There is none that understandeth, there is none that seeketh after God. ¹² They are all gone out of the way, they are together become unprofitable; there is none that doeth good, no, not one. ¹³ Their throat *is* an open sepulchre; with their tongues they have used deceit; the poison of asps is under their lips: 14 Whose mouth *is* full of cursing and bitterness: ¹⁵ Their feet *are swift* to shed blood: ¹⁶ Destruction and misery *are* in their ways: ¹⁷ And the war: of peace have they not known: ¹⁸ There is no fear of God before their eyes.

Rom 3:22-23
Even the righteousness of God *which is* by faith of Jesus Christ unto all and upon all them that believe: for there is no difference: ²³ For all have sinned, and come short of the glory of God;

For every one that doeth evil hateth the light, neither cometh to the light, lest his deeds should be reproved. [21] But he that doeth truth cometh to the light, that his deeds may be made manifest, that they are wrought in God.

1John 3:18
He that believeth on him is not condemned: but he that believeth not is condemned already, because he hath not believed in the name of the only begotten Son of God.

Eph 2:8-9
For by grace are ye saved through faith; and that not of yourselves: *it is* the gift of God: [9] Not of works, lest any man should boast.

Yes, but I keep the Ten Commandments!
Rom 3:20
Therefore by the deeds of the law there shall no flesh be justified in his sight: for by the law is the knowledge of sin.

The same thing is told in Galatians.
Gal 3:11
But that no man is justified by the law in the sight of God, *it is* evident: for, the just shall live by faith.

With out the shedding of blood there is no remission of sin.

Heb 9:22 And almost all things are by the law purged with blood; and without shedding of blood is no remission.

Rom 5:6 For when we were yet without strength, in due time Christ died for the ungodly.

Isa 53:6 All we like sheep have gone astray; we have turned every one to his own way; and the LORD hath laid on him the iniquity of us all.

1 Pet 1:18-19
Forasmuch as ye know that ye were not redeemed with corruptible things, as silver and gold, from your vain conversation *received* by tradition from your fathers; [19] But with the precious blood of Christ, as of a lamb without blemish and without spot:

Should I repent for my sins?
Acts 17:30 And the times of this ignorance God winked at; but now commandeth all men every where to repent:

Luke 13:3 I tell you, Nay: but, except ye repent, ye shall all likewise perish.

2 Cor 7:10
For godly sorrow worketh repentance to salvation not to be repented of but the sorrow of the world worketh death.

May I be saved or receive salvation immediately?
Luke 19:6-9
And he made haste, and came down, and received him joyfully. 7 And when they saw *it,* they all murmured, saying, That he was gone to be guest with a man that is a sinner. [8] And Zacchaeus stood, and said unto the Lord; Behold, Lord, the half of my goods I give to the poor; and if have taken any thing from any man by false accusation, I restore *him* fourfold. [9] And Jesus said unto him, This day is salvation come to this house, forsomuch as he also is a son of Abraham.

Acts 10:44-48
While Peter yet spake these words, the Holy Ghost fell on all then which heard the word. [45] And they of the circumcision which believe were astonished, as many as came with Peter, because that on the Gentiles also was poured out the gift of the Holy Ghost. [46] For they heard them speak with tongues, and magnify God. Then answered Peter 47 Can any man forbid water, that these should not be baptized, which have received the Holy Ghost as well as we? [48]

And he commanded them to be baptized in the name of the Lord. Then prayed they him to tarry certain days.

Luke 23:42-43
And he said unto Jesus, Lord, remember me when thou comest into thy kingdom. [43] And Jesus said unto him, Verily I say unto thee, To day shalt thou be with me in paradise.

Do I need to pray to get saved?
Rom 10:12
For there is no difference between the Jew and the Greek: for the same Lord over all is rich unto all that call upon him.

What about public confession?
Mat 10:32
Whosoever therefore shall confess me before men, him will I confess also before my Father which is in heaven.

Rom 10:9
That if thou shalt confess with thy mouth the Lord Jesus, and shalt believe in thine heart that God hath raised him from the dead, thou shalt be saved.

Rom 10:10
For with the heart man believeth unto righteousness; and with the mouth confession is made unto salvation.

What did Jesus say he would do if you came to Him?
John 6:37
All that the Father giveth me shall come to me; and him that cometh to me I will in no wise cast out.

John 1:12
But as many as received him, to them gave he power to become the sons of God, *even* to them that believe on his name:

If you are a sinner, believe on the Lord Jesus Christ.
Acts 16:31
And they said, Believe on the Lord Jesus Christ, and thou shalt be saved, and thy house.

What must I do if I sin after I am saved?
1 John 1:9
If we confess our sins, he is faithful and just to forgive us *our* sins, and to cleanse us from all unrighteousness.

Prov 28:13
He that covereth his sins shall not prosper: but whoso confesseth and forsaketh *them* shall have mercy.

What if I don't know the Word like others?
2 Tim 2:15
Study to show thyself approved unto God, a workman that needeth no to be ashamed, rightly dividing the word of truth.

James 1:5
If any of you lack wisdom, let him ask of God, that giveth to all *men* liberally, and upbraideth not; and it shall be given him.

Josh 1:8
This book of the law shall not depart out of thy mouth; but thou shalt meditate therein day and night, that thou mayest observe to do according to all that is written therein: for then thou shalt make thy way prosperous, and then thou shalt have good success.

CHAPTER 7

What Must I Do To Be Saved?

In the last session of this lesson, let us recap what we have learned about how to be saved.

What Must I Do To Be Saved?
Without a shadow of doubt you can be saved according to the Word of God.
1. There is no other name (JESUS) where by we must be saved.
2. Jesus is the only way to the Father.
3. Jesus is the only way unto Eternal Life.
4. Jesus is the only sacrifice for our sins
5. Jesus is the Author of Eternal Salvation.
6. Jesus is the only way to Peace.
7. Jesus is the Resurrection and the Life.

The Lord has given a commandment and an invitation.
Mat 28:19-20
Go ye therefore, and teach all nations, baptizing them in the name of the Father, and of the Son, and of the Holy Ghost: [20] Teaching them to observe all things whatsoever I have commanded you: and, lo, I am with you alway, *even* unto the end of the world. Amen.

Mark 16:15-16
And he said unto them, Go ye into all the world, and preach the gospel to every creature. [16] He that believeth and is baptized shall be saved; but he that believeth not shall be damned.

Acts 2:38-39
Then Peter said unto them, Repent, and be baptized every one of you in the name of Jesus Christ for the remission of sins, and ye shall

receive the gift of the Holy Ghost. [39] For the promise is unto you, and to your children, and to all that are afar off, *even* as many as the Lord our God shall call.

John 1:12
But as many as received him, to them gave he power to become the sons of God, *even* to them that believe on his name:

John 3:14-16
And as Moses lifted up the serpent in the wilderness, even so must the Son of man be lifted up: [15] That whosoever believeth in him should not perish, but have eternal life. [16] For God so loved the world, that he gave his only begotten Son, that whosoever believeth in him should not perish, but have everlasting life.

John 3:18
He that believeth on him is not condemned: but he that believeth not is condemned already, because he hath not believed in the name of the only begotten Son of God.

John 3:36
He that believeth on the Son hath everlasting life: and he that believeth not the Son shall not see life; but the wrath of God abideth on him.
John 5:24
Verily, verily, I say unto you, He that heareth my word, and believeth on him that sent me, hath everlasting life, and shall not come into condemnation; but is passed from death unto life.

John 6:40
And this is the will of him that sent me, that every one which seeth the Son, and believeth on him, may have everlasting life: and I will raise him up at the last day.

John 6:47
Verily, verily, I say unto you, He that believeth on me hath everlasting life.

Acts 10:43
To him give all the prophets witness, that through his name whosoever believeth in him shall receive remission of sins.

Acts 13:39
And by him all that believe are justified from all things, from which ye could not be justified by the Law of Moses.

What Must I Do To Be Saved?
Acts 16:30-31
And brought them out, and said, Sirs, what must I do to be saved? ³¹ And they said, Believe on the Lord Jesus Christ, and thou shalt be saved, and thy house.

Prayer to receive Salvation
Father, in the name of Jesus I believe in my heart and confess with my mouth that Jesus is the Messiah the Son of the true and living God. I believe that Jesus is the Savior, who died on the cross for the sin of the world and mine. Therefore, I ask in the name of Jesus that you forgive me for all of my sins, willful and secret sins. Father I also believe in the death, burial and resurrection of Jesus Christ according to the Holy Scriptures. Heavenly Father, I believe in Jesus in my heart and confess Him with my mouth, and receive Him as my Lord, my Savior, and mighty God. Thank you Father in the Name of Jesus Christ for my salvation. Amen.

This prayer when prayed with a singleness of heart, mind, and purpose to receive Jesus Christ as your Lord and Savior will result in *salvation* and *eternal life*. In other words your *faith*, and *confessions* made in the "salvation prayer" is what it takes to be saved, born again, the new birth, salvation and eternal life. Moreover, this starts the regeneration work of the Holy Spirit for *salvation* and *eternal life*.

The regeneration work of the Holy Spirit will result in baptizing born again believers into the body of Christ. First Corinthians 13 says: *"For by one Spirit are we all baptized into one body, whether we be Jews or Gentiles, whether we be bond or free; and have been all made to drink into one Spirit."* This is the "one baptism into the body of Christ." At this time a believer is translated from the kingdom of Satan into the kingdom of His Son-the Body of Christ. Believes are emerged into the Body of Christ and indwelled by the Holy Spirit at the time of the new birth. The Holy Spirit then began a progressive work in the life of the believer. The Holy Spirit progressively leads, guides, teaches convicts, inspires, and keeps the believer.

The scriptures studied in this book are overwhelming clear about what the Bible teaches about *salvation and life.* In them you saw words like, "believe," "repent," "confess," "be baptized," call on the name of Jesus," and according to Acts 16:31; *"Believe on the Lord Jesus Christ, and thou shalt be saved. And thy house.*

Prayer to receive the Baptism with the Holy Ghost

Most Holy and everlasting Father: in the name of Jesus Christ my Lord and savior. I pray thee master that thou would hear my plea. I pray thee that thou would cleanse me, and purge me of all sins and unrighteousness. Bless me now Lord, that I may worship you in spirit and truth. I surrender my all unto you. Take me and use me Lord in thy service, according to thy own will and purpose. Lord I believe the Holy Scriptures concerning the receiving and baptism with the Holy Ghost. For it is written in the Holy scriptures with promise: to those who believe on the Lord Jesus. Therefore Lord, I desire with all my heart, praying, and asking thee that I receive the promise of the Father. Fill me Lord with this Gift for it is promised unto all thy people.

Lord I desire to receive the Baptism with the Holy Ghost with all my heart. I desire to receive even as the Samaritans did who believed and was baptized at the preaching of Philip and the laying on of hands of Peter and John.

I pray oh Lord that I may be baptized with the Hold Ghost even as the Gentiles received at Cornelius house at the preaching of Peter. I pray to receive even as the twelve disciples of John the Baptist who received the Baptism with the Holy Ghost at the preaching of Paul in Ephesus. Lord, they spoke in tongues glorifying thee, magnifying thee and prophesying in thy name.

Even so Lord, I desire to receive, for it is written in the scriptures… "If any man thirst, let him come unto me, and drink." "Lord it is also written…" "If ye then, being evil, know how to give good gifts unto your children; how much more shall your heavenly Father give the Holy Spirit to them that ask Him?"

I pray the Lord Jesus for this Blessed Gift. In thy name; I now expect to receive the Baptism with the Holy Ghost with boldness and power. Impart unto me Spiritual Gifts, that I may work the works of Jesus Christ. In the name of Jesus manifest thy glory in me, and use me in thy service. Amen.

He shall baptize you with the Holy Ghost
Luke 3:16
John answered, saying unto them all, I indeed baptize you with water; but one mightier than I cometh, the latchet of whose shoes I am not worthy to unloose: he shall baptize you with the Holy Ghost and with fire:

John declared who will baptize with the Holy Ghost
John 1:33
And I knew him not: but he that sent me to baptize with water, the same said unto me, upon whom thou shalt see the Spirit descending, and remaining on him, the same is he which baptizeth with the Holy Ghost.

Jesus promise the Holy Ghost and Power
Acts 1:5,8
For John truly baptized with water; but ye shall be baptized with the Holy Ghost not many days hence**…But ye shall receive power, after that the Holy Ghost is come upon you**: and ye shall be witnesses unto me both in Jerusalem, and in all Judaea, and in Samaria, and unto the uttermost part of the earth.

Ovit G. Pursley, Sr.

Jesus acquire the Holy Ghost
Acts 2:32-33
This Jesus hath God raised up, whereof we all are witnesses. [33] Therefore being by the right hand of God exalted, and having received of the Father the promise of the Holy Ghost, he hath shed forth this, which ye now see and hear.
The Holy Ghost promise to all believers
Acts 2:38-39
Then Peter said unto them, Repent, and be baptized every one of you in the name of Jesus Christ for the remission of sins, and ye shall receive the gift of the Holy Ghost. [39] For the promise is unto you, and today to your children, and to all that are afar off even as many as the Lord our God shall call.

Again, we notice that the scriptures just mention has very little to say about being born again, or eternal life. You will have to agree that these scriptures are talking about the *"Promise of the Father,"* the Baptism with the Holy Ghost for POWER and SERVICE. Supernatural Power and the Anointing must accompany the Word: to work the works, of Christ. In other words, you cannot have signs, wonders and miracles happening in your church service on regular bases without the Supernatural Power and the Anointing of the Holy Spirit.

CHAPTER 8

Seven Steps to Holy Ghost Power

Let me speak more to the point. Do you seriously want to receive power, the baptism with the Holy Ghost? If you answer is yes, then there are seven things (**Note: The Bible does not teach seven things for you to do. But, there are _seven_ things**) that you can do, to line *your faith, confession and your spirit up with the word of God* that you may receive the Baptism with the Holy Ghost, **"The Promise of POWER."**

Acts 2:38 Then Peter said unto them, Repent, and be baptized ever one of you in the name of Jesus Christ for the remission o sins, and ye shall receive the gift of the Holy Ghost.

John 3:16
For God so loved the world, that he gave his only begotten Son, that whosoever believeth in him should not perish, but have everlasting life.

Make sure you are saved first.
First step: *Believe on Jesus;* put your faith entirely in Him for what He has done for salvation and life. We are to rest absolutely on what He has already done (John 3:16-17).

Second Step: *Repentance,* even if you are already saved, born again; repent of all willful and secret sins. Remember Jesus is our example; even though He was with out sin, He humble Himself to the will of the Father (Acts 2:38).

51

Acts 2:38
Then Peter said unto them, Repent, and he baptized even one of you in the name of Jesus Christ for the remission o sins, and ye shall receive the gift of the Holy Ghost.

Third Step: *Confession and Obedience,* Jesus humble Himself and God exalted Him (Luke 3:21-22). Likewise, we must humble ourselves to make an open confession before the Lord and the world of our renunciation of sin and our acceptance of Jesus Christ, by baptism. Our faith and hope must depend entirely upon the redemptive work of Jesus Christ.

It is important to understand that the baptism with the Holy Ghost may precede water baptism. In fact, many have come forward to be saved, and received the Baptism with the Holy Spirit the same day or night they got saved. This was the case with the household of Cornelius (Acts 10:44-47).

Mat 10:32
Whosoever therefore shall confess me before men, him will I confess also before my Father which is in heaven.

Eph 2:8-9
For by grace are ye saved through faith; and that not of yourselves: it is the gift of God. 9 Not of works, lest any man should boast.

Titus 3:5
Not by works of righteousness which we have done, but according to his mercy he saved us, by the washing of regeneration, and renewing of the Holy Ghost;

Obedience, to God's will, means a total surrender to all that He commands; to obey Him in all things. This is clearly implied in Acts 2:38, but it is brought out more explicitly in Acts 5:32 *"32And we are his witnesses of these things; and so is also the Holy Ghost, whom God hath given to them that obey him."*

Forth Step: *Surrender,* to the will of God. We must surrender our whole body, soul, and spirit to God. Let the Holy Spirit have His way in your life.

Romans 8:32

32He that spared not his own Son, but delivered him up for us all how shall he not with him also freely give us all things?

Psalms 84:11

"For the LORD God is a sun and shield. the LORD will give grace and glory: no good thing will he withhold from them that walk uprightly.

Fifth Step: *Thirst,* we must desire to be filled. One should have a deep hunger and thirst to be baptized with the Holy Ghost. (John 7:37-39; Isaiah 44:3; Matthew 5:6; 6:33).

John 7:37-39

37In the last day, that great day of the feast, Jesus stood and cried, saying, If any man thirst, let him come unto me, and drink. 38He that believeth on me, as the scripture hath said, out of his belly shall flow rivers of living water. 39(But this. spake he of the Spirit, which they that believe on him should receive: for the Holy Ghost was not yet given; because than Jesus was not yet glorified.)

Sixth Step: *Prayer,* one of the most basic principles of God's word is *prayer. Simply* go to God in prayer and ask Him to baptize you with the Holy Ghost. Remember, the Holy Spirit was given to the church as a whole at Pentecost, but each individual must still appropriate the gift for himself.

Luke 11:13

[13]*If ye then, being evil, know how to give good gifts unto your children. how much more shall your heavenly Father give the Holy Spirit to them that ask him?*

Seventh Step: *Faith,* again one of the basic principles of God's word is *faith.* Our duty is to simply believe God's word and act accordingly. We may not understand some things about God's word but we are to simply believe.

James 1:6-7
⁶But let him ask in faith, nothing wavering. For he that wavereth is like a wave of the sea driven with the wind and tossed. ⁷For let not that man think that he shall receive any thing of the Lord.

1 John 5:14
14And this is the confidence that we have in him, that, if we ask any thing according to his will, he heareth us:

WE should expect Jesus to keep His promise and baptize us with the Holy Ghost (Mark 11:24; Acts 1:4-5).

CHAPTER 9

Principles of Salvation

I   **Come to Jesus to learn the way of Salvation.**
1. The way of salvation is based on Christ's death; 1 Corinthians 5:1-4.
2. The way of salvation is revealed in the Gospels; John 5:24.
3. The way of salvation is plainly revealed; John 3:16.

II   **Come to Jesus for the forgiveness of sin.**
1. The forgiveness of sin is through Christ's blood; Ephesians 1:7.
2. The forgiveness of sin is through Christ; Romans 10:9-10.
3. The forgiveness of sin through Christ is complete; Colossians 2:13.

III   **One should have faith that is personal.**
1. A personal faith in Christ is needed; Hebrews 11:6.
2. A personal faith in Christ is to be desired; Acts 16:30.
3. A personal faith in Christ brings everlasting life; John 6:40, 47.
4. Faith without works is dead; James 2:20.
5. Faith that works helps the brethren; III John 1:5.
6. Faith that works produces peace Romans 15:13.

IV   **You must be born from above.**
1. To be born from above is to become a child of God; John 1:12.
2. To be born from above is to have a divine nature; II Peter 1:4.
3. To be born from above is to be accepted in the beloved; Ephesians 1:6.

V   God's Grace is sufficient to prove His love and provide salvation.
1. Grace is the source of God's love. 1 John 4:10.
2. Grace brings God's love; 1 Timothy 1:14.
3. Grace is to all who love the Lord Jesus Christ; Ephesians 6:24.
4. Salvation is by grace through faith; Ephesians 2:8, 9.
5. Salvation, forgiveness of sin, is by the riches of His grace; Ephesians 1:7.
6. Salvation is through the loving grace of the Lord Jesus; Acts 15:11.

VI   What's the importance of Christ's mission to the world?
1. Christ came to reveal God's love; 1 John 4:8,9.
2. Christ came to offer God's salvation; Acts 4:12.
3. Christ came to make life on earth more abundant; John 10:10.

VII   Jesus mission on earth.
1. He came to preach; Mark 1:3,8.
2. He came to fulfill the law; Matthew 5:17.
3. He came to save sinners; 1 Timothy 1:15.
4. He came to give and abundant life; John 10:10.
5. He came to heal the sick, set the captive free, and to set at liberty those that are bruised; Luke 4:17,18.

VIII   Christ is the only way to salvation
1. Christ is the captain of our salvation; Hebrews 2:10.
2. Christ was exalted to give salvation; Acts 5:31.
3. Christ is the only way to the Father; John 14:6.
4. There is no escape to those who neglect salvation; Hebrews 2:3.
5. The day of salvation is now; Isaiah 49:8.
6. There is no second chance of salvation after death; Luke 16:24, 26.

CHAPTER 10

HELL: Will You Be There?

¹⁹There was a certain rich man, which was clothed in purple and fine linen, and fared sumptuously every day: ²⁰And there was a certain beggar named Lazarus, which was laid at his gate, full of sores, ²¹And desiring to be fed with the crumbs which fell from the rich man's table: moreover the dogs came and licked his sores. ²²And it came to pass, that the beggar died, and was carried by the angels into Abraham's bosom: the rich man also died, and was buried; ²³And in hell he lift up his eyes, being in torments, and seeth Abraham afar off, and Lazarus in his bosom. ²⁴And he cried and said, Father Abraham, have mercy on me, and send Lazarus, that he may dip the tip of his finger in water, and cool my tongue; for I am tormented in this flame. ²⁵But Abraham said, Son, remember that thou in thy lifetime receivedst thy good things, and likewise Lazarus evil things: but now he is comforted, and thou art tormented. ²⁶And beside all this, between us and you there is a great gulf fixed: so that they which would pass from hence to you cannot; neither can they pass to us, that *would come* from thence. ²⁷Then he said, I pray thee therefore, father, that thou wouldest send him to my father's house: ²⁸For I have five brethren; that he may testify unto them, lest they also come into this place of torment. ²⁹Abraham saith unto him, they have Moses and the prophets; let them hear them. ³⁰And he said, Nay, father Abraham: but if one went unto them from the dead, they will repent. ³¹And he said unto him, If they hear not Moses and the prophets, neither will they be persuaded, though one rose from the dead.

-Luke 16:19-31

Ovit G. Pursley, Sr.

There is a real Devil and a real Hell
The New Testament gives us many names of Satan, thereby providing insight into his malevolence.

Names of Satan
1. Abaddon ------------------------- Revelation 9:11
2. Accuser --------------------------- Revelation 12:10
3. Adversary ------------------------- Peter 5:8
4. Apollyon -------------------------- Revelation 9:11
5. Beelzebub ------------------------- Matthew 12:24
6. Belial ------------------------------ 2 Corinthians 6:15
7. Devil ------------------------------- Matthew 4:1
8. Enemy ----------------------------- Matthew 13:28
9. Evil One --------------------------- John 17:15
10. God of this World --------------- 2 Corinthians 4:4
11. Liar -------------------------------- John 8:44
12. Murderer ------------------------- John 8:44
13. Prince of the Power of the Air-- Ephesians 2:2
14. Red Dragon ---------------------- Revelation 12:3, 7, 9
15. Ruler of this World ------------- John 12:31
16. Satan ----------------------------- Matthew 4:10
17. Serpent of Old ------------------- Revelation 12:9
18. Tempter -------------------------- Matthew 4:3

There Is a Real Hell
Ways the Bible Describes Hell
There are many biblical descriptions of hell—eternal separation from God---are seriously sobering.
1. Flaming fire ---------------------- 2 Thessalonians 1:7-8
2. This flame ------------------------ Luke 16:24
3. Unquenchable fire --------------- Matthew 3:12; Luke 3:17
4. Everlasting fire ------------------- Matthew 18:8; 25:41
5. Hell fire --------------------------- Matthew 5:22; Mark 9:47
6. Furnace of fire ------------------- Matthew 13:42, 50
7. Lake of fire ----------------------- Revelation 19:20; 20:10, 14-15; 21:8

Other Descriptions of Hell

1. The worm does not die   Mark 9:48
2. Shame and everlasting contempt   Daniel 12:2
3. A place of destruction   Matthew 7:13; Philippians 3:19
4. A place of weeping and gnashing of teeth   Matthew 13:42, 50; 22:13
5. Everlasting punishment   Matthew 25:46; Jude 1:7
6. Outer Darkness   Matthew 8:12; 22:13
7. The wrath to come   Luke 3:7; Romans 5:9; 1 Thessalonians 1:10
8. A place of torment   Luke 16:28; Revelation 14:11; 20:10
9. Everlasting destruction   2 Thessalonians 1:9
10. A place of damnation or condemnation   Jude 1:4
11. A place of retribution   2 Corinthians 11:15
12. The second death   Revelation 20:14; 21:8

YES! The Bible Speaks About Hell!

My Friend, do all that you can do to stay out of this place call HELL.

Want you call on the Name of the Lord Jesus Christ TODAY?

Ask the Lord to save you. Believe on Him in your heart and confess Him with your mouth and you shall be saved.

More about the place call Hell ... And it's not a good place to be.
2 Peter 2:4 – 6

⁴For if God spared not the angels that sinned, but cast *them* down to hell, and delivered *them* into chains of darkness, to be reserved unto judgment; ⁵And spared not the old world, but saved Noah the eighth *person*, a preacher of righteousness, bringing in the flood upon the world of the ungodly; ⁶And turning the cities of Sodom and Gomorrha into ashes condemned *them* with an overthrow, making *them* an ensample unto those that after should live ungodly;

2 Peter 2:7 – 9

⁷And delivered just Lot, vexed with the filthy conversation of the wicked: ⁸(For that righteous man dwelling among them, in seeing and hearing, vexed *his* righteous soul from day to day with *their* unlawful deeds;) ⁹The Lord knoweth how to deliver the godly out of temptations, and to reserve the unjust unto the day of judgment to be punished:

Luke 12:5

⁵But I will forewarn you whom ye shall fear: Fear him, which after he hath killed hath power to cast into hell; yea, I say unto you, Fear him

2 Peter 2:4 – 6

⁴For if God spared not the angels that sinned, but cast *them* down to hell, and delivered *them* into chains of darkness, to be reserved unto judgment; ⁵And spared not the old world, but saved Noah the eighth *person*, a preacher of righteousness, bringing in the flood upon the world of the ungodly; ⁶And turning the cities of Sodom and Gomorrha into ashes condemned *them* with an overthrow, making *them* an ensample unto those that after should live ungodly.

Deuteronomy 32:22

²²For a fire is kindled in mine anger, and shall burn unto the lowest hell, and shall consume the earth with her increase, and set on fire the foundations of the mountains.

Psalms 9:17

The wicked shall be turned into hell, *and* all the nations that forget God.

Psalms 139:8

⁸ If I ascend up into heaven, thou *art* there: if I make my bed in hell, behold, thou *art there.*

Psalms 115:11

¹¹ Ye that fear the LORD, trust in the LORD: he *is* their help and their shield

Proverbs 15:11

¹¹Hell and destruction *are* before the LORD: how much more then the hearts of the children of men?

Proverbs 27:20

²⁰Hell and destruction are never full; so the eyes of man are never satisfied

Isaiah 5:14

¹⁴Therefore hell hath enlarged herself, and opened her mouth without measure: and their glory, and their multitude, and their pomp, and he that rejoiceth, shall descend into it.

Matthew 5:22

²²But I say unto you, that whosoever is angry with his brother without a cause shall be in danger of the judgment: and whosoever shall say to his brother, Raca, shall be in danger of the council: but whosoever shall say, Thou fool, shall be in danger of hell fire.

Matthew 10:28

²⁸And fear not them which kill the body, but are not able to kill the soul: but rather fear him which is able to destroy both soul and body in hell.

Matthew 16:18 - 19

¹⁸And I say also unto thee, that thou art Peter, and upon this rock I will build my church; and the gates of hell shall not prevail against it. ¹⁹And I will give unto thee the keys of the kingdom of heaven: and whatsoever thou shalt bind on earth shall be bound in heaven: and whatsoever thou shalt loose on earth shall be loosed in heaven.

Revelation 1:18 - 19
[18]I *am* he that liveth, and was dead; and, behold, I am alive for evermore, Amen; and have the keys of hell and of death. [19]Write the things which thou hast seen, and the things which are, and the things which shall be hereafter;

Revelation 6:8 - 9
[8]And I looked, and behold a pale horse: and his name that sat on him was Death, and Hell followed with him. And power was given unto them over the fourth part of the earth, to kill with sword, and with hunger, and with death, and with the beasts of the earth. [9]And when he had opened the fifth seal, I saw under the altar the souls of them that were slain for the word of God, and for the testimony which they held:

Revelation 20:11 – 12
[11]And I saw a great white throne, and him that sat on it, from whose face the earth and the heaven fled away; and there was found no place for them. [12]And I saw the dead, small and great, stand before God; and the books were opened: and another book was opened, which is *the book* of life: and the dead were judged out of those things which were written in the books, according to their works.

Revelation 20:13
[13]And the sea gave up the dead which were in it; and death and hell delivered up the dead which were in them: and they were judged every man according to their works.

Revelation 20:14 – 15
[14]And death and hell were cast into the lake of fire. This is the second death. [15]And whosoever was not found written in the book of life was cast into the lake of fire.

What you can do to keep from going to Hell
Believe on Jesus, Repent of your sins, Confess you faith in Jesus, and
the word of God, Receive Jesus as your Lord and savior, be baptized,
Unite with a local church, Give of your means to support the work
of the Lord, Study the word of God, and continue in God's word.

1. Have faith in God, the Lord Jesus Christ.
2. Hear the Word of God.
3. Believe the Word of God.
4. Receive the Word of God.
5. Confess the Word of God.
6. Repent of your sins.
7. Receive Jesus Christ as Lord and Savior.
8. Be Baptized in the name of the Father, Son and the Holy Ghost.
9. Unite with a local (church) fellowship of Believers.
10. Give of your means unto the work of the Lord.
11. Study to show thyself approved unto God.
12. Continue in God's Word.

Pray the prayer of salvation
*Father, in the name of Jesus, I believe in my heart and confess
with my mouth that Jesus is the Messiah the Son of the true
and living God. I believe that Jesus is the Savior, who died on
the cross for the sin of the world and mine. Therefore, I ask in
the name of Jesus that you forgive me for all of my sins, willful
and secret sins. Father I also believe in the death, burial and
resurrection of Jesus Christ according to the Holy Scriptures.
Heavenly Father, I believe in Jesus in my heart and confess Him
with my mouth, and receive Him as my Lord, my Savior, and
mighty God. Thank you Father in the Name of Jesus Christ for
my salvation. Amen.*

Ovit G. Pursley, Sr.

Words of encouragement
We are not saved by: *"Works of righteousness which we have done."*

Titus 3:5-6
Not by works of righteousness which we have done, but according to his mercy he saved us, by the washing of regeneration, and renewing of the Holy Ghost; Tit 3:6 Which he shed on us abundantly through Jesus Christ our Saviour.

Hebrews 4:16 Let us therefore come boldly unto the throne of grace that we may obtain mercy, and find grace to help in time of need.

Hebrews 11:6 But without faith it is impossible to please him: for he that cometh to God must believe that he is, and that he is a rewarder of them that diligently seek him.

James 1:12 Blessed is the man that endureth temptation: for when he is tried, he shall receive the crown of life, which the Lord hath promised to them that love him.

James 1:22 But be ye doers of the word, and not hearers only, deceiving your own selves.

James 4:7 Submit yourselves therefore to God. Resist the devil, and he will flee from you.

1 Peter 1:3-4
Blessed be the God and Father of our Lord Jesus Christ, which according to his abundant mercy hath begotten us again unto a lively hope by the resurrection of Jesus Christ from the dead, 4 To an inheritance incorruptible, and undefiled, and that fadeth not away, reserved in heaven for you.

1 Peter 2:2 As newborn babes, desire the sincere milk of the word, that ye may grow thereby:

1 Peter 3:15 But sanctify the Lord God in your hearts: and be ready always to give an answer to every man that asketh you a reason of the hope that is in you with meekness and fear.

1 Peter 5:6-7 Humble yourselves therefore under the mighty hand of God, that he may exalt you in due time: 7 Casting all your care upon him; for he careth for you.

2 Peter 1:3 According as his divine power hath given unto us all things that pertain unto life and godliness, through the knowledge of him that hath called us to glory and virtue.

1 John 1:9 If we confess our sins, he is faithful and just to forgive us our sins, and to cleanse us from all unrighteousness.

1 John 2:15 Love not the world, neither the things that are in the world. If any man love the world, the love of the Father is not in him.

1 John 5:11-12 And this is the record that God hath given to us eternal life, and this life is in his Son. 12 He that hath the Son hath life; and he that hath not the Son of God hath not life.

1 John 5:13 These things have I written unto you that believe on the name of the Son of God; that ye may know that ye have eternal life, and that ye may believe on the name of the Son of God.

Revelation 3:20 Behold, I stand at the door, and knock: if any man hear my voice, and open the door, I will come in to him, and will sup with him, and he with me.

Hebrews 2:3-4
3How shall we escape, if we neglect so great salvation; which at the first began to be spoken by the Lord, and was confirmed unto us by them that heard him; 4God also bearing them witness, both with signs and wonders, and with divers miracles, and gifts of the Holy Ghost, according to his own will?

Notes

Notes

Ovit G. Pursley Ministries®

Sow a Seed Today

*"...Pay thy vows unto the most high and call upon me in the day of trouble;" I will deliver thee...*Psalm: 50:14-15

Jesus is coming soon!

This is a good work, anointed of the Lord Jesus Christ.
Note: All Glory, Honor, Praise, and Thanksgiving is given unto God the Father, the Lord Jesus Christ, and the Holy Spirit for the knowledge and wisdom to compile all books by *Ovit G. Pursley Ministries.*

Ovit G. Pursley Ministries Publishes Books, Bible studies for the Christian Market. The mission is to save, teach, strengthen, and establish believers in the faith. To provide a way for Ministers and Lay people to know Christ and make -Him known by publishing life-related materials that are Biblically rooted and: culturally reverent.

Ovit G. Pursley Personal Commission: "Go save, confirm, strengthen and establish believers in the Faith. Ministering both to the Spiritual and Physical needs of God's people, especially those who are starving for the sincere milk and meat of the Word. And lo I am with you always."

NOTICE: To Pastors, Ministers, Church Groups or Bible Study Groups; you may order in bulk (Large number of books for your congregation or study group). When doing so we recommend that you collect all money for each book and write a (one) check from the church or study group for the order. Thank You! Make your order TODAY!!!

Do something before it's too late!!!

Help me bless the body of Christ!
Sow a Seed Today!

Note: All Gifts, Love Offerings, Contributions, and Seed Sowing into this Ministry are highly appreciated to support this great work of God for the Body of Christ.

❑ I believe this is a work anointed of God! My Seed- Gift is:
❑ $50 ❑ $100 ❑ $200 ❑ $500 ❑ $1,000 ❑ $_____
❑ Enclosed is $ _____toward *my* Vow of Faith.

Please make all checks and money orders payable in (U.S. FUNDS ONLY) to *Ovit G. Pursley Ministries* and send order with remittance to:

Ovit G. Pursley Ministries
11130 Kingston Pike, Ste. 103
Knoxville, Tennessee 37934

"Give, and it shall be given unto you; good measure, pressed down, and shaken together, and running over, shall men give into your bosom. For with the same measure that ye mete withal it shall be measured to you again." Luke 6:38

Those wishing to contact Elder Ovit Pursley personally for *Special Prayer, Contributions or to Sow Seed into this Ministry* may write in care of the following address:

Ovit G. Pursley Ministries
11130 Kingston Pike, Ste. 103
Knoxville, TN 37934

*Feel free to copy this page to send with your seed offering!
Name: _____
Address: _____
City: _____ State_____ Zip: _____
Email: _____
Phone: (   ) _____ Cell: (   ) _____

Ovit & Patricia Pursley, Sr.

About The Author

Ovit G. Pursley Sr. is a chosen vessel, called, and ordained of God to preach and teach the Gospel of Jesus Christ, and to minister to the spiritual and physical needs of His people.

He is anointed in the Five-Fold Ministry (Apostle, Pastor, Teacher, Prophet, and Evangelist); Healing, and Deliverance. He is a "Powerful Word Preacher, Teacher, and Evangelist," who proclaims; that the Power of God unto Salvation is in the "Word" the "Holy Spirit," the "Name and Blood of Jesus and the Resurrection of Jesus Christ."

He served as the senior Pastor of the Oak Grove Missionary Baptist Church of Niota, Tennessee for 14 years. He also served one (I) year as Second Vice Moderator and seven (7) years as First Vice Moderator of the Loudon District Baptist Missionary and Education Association. He also served ten (10) years as a National Evangelist. Presently: fulfilling his mission as a writer of the living word.